TO LOVE AN ISLAND

ANA PORTNOY BRIMMER

To Love an Island

YESYES BOOKS

Cover art: "MAY DAY 2018" by Colectivo Moriví (2018), Boriken Me Llama Art
Series, acrylic paint over Masonite, Segundo Ruiz Belvis Cultural Center, Chicago, IL
Interior art: "Estado de Emergencia" © 2019 BEMBA PR
Cover & Interior Design: Alban Fischer

ISBN 978-1-936919-87-1
Printed in the United States of America

Published by YesYes Books
1614 NE Alberta St
Portland, OR 97211
yesyesbooks.com

KMA Sullivan, Publisher
Stevie Edwards, Senior Editor, Book Development
Alban Fischer, Graphic Designer
Cole Hildebrand, Managing Editor
Alexis Smithers, Assistant Editor
Amber Rambharose, Assistant Editor, Instagram
James Sullivan, Assistant Editor, Audio Books
Phillip B. Williams, Coeditor In Chief, Vinyl
Amie Zimmerman, Events Coordinator

"My homeland! The iron of my chains is teaching me
The vulture's violence, and the optimist's fragility
I did not know that beneath our skin
Is the birth of a storm . . ."

Mahmoud Darwish
translated by Mohammad Shaheen

"*y en todo somos independientes,
hasta en el hueco más colonizado del temor poroso;
hasta en la panadería más llena de periódicos de anuncios;
hasta en el acto corrosivo de decir que somos isla solamente*"

Raquel Salas Rivera

"*Somos más y no tenemos miedo*"

Puerto Rico

Contents

Strawberries

I'd always been told strawberries couldn't grow
in Puerto Rico. We didn't have the climate.

> Up here on this finca, past the carcass
> of Peñuelas's petroleum past, where even

the hummingbirds are dizzy with height,
small strawberry studs slip off like beads

> from a necklace on my tongue. The farmer picks
> them gently from their fuzzy casing—warm

and tender from swallowing the world's
beatings—as he shows us his budding coffee crop.

> *Crecemos el café bajo sombra.*
> I think of all the work we do in the shadows.

Rearing coffee under the sun is hurried
and stifles taste. Its flavor should be layered

> like the rock that makes this mountain,
> this mountain of an island.

All plants are carbon-husked patience.
But coffee is a slow birth, bean of push

that can take as long as four years to ripen.
Intercropped with bananas, papayas, and pyrethrum

to lure away pests, allow for just and solidary
growth, an abundant existence—this steep hill

of harvest is everything we're slowly trying to become.
The farmer says after the hurricane, they lost

the majority of their coffee shrubs.
Seeds were swept away with all else.

Mass growers strike deals and offer seeds
so local farmers can grow to sell back to them.

We have to grow our own to be our own,
he smiles, splits open a coffee pod

drops the pulpy body
in my hand and tells me to try it.

I'd always been told freedom would never come
for Puerto Rico. We didn't have the climate.

I ask the farmer about the strawberries. *Son silvestres,*
he responds, and points to their beautiful excess.

Breathing Up Storms

A hurricane has come and gone.
What do we tell our children now?

Tell them about the waters. The ones they wade
      in, taste on their lips. Tell them not to fear the waves

that baptized them. That heat grows
      like a fetus, and come June, another swell will miscarry

into the wind. Tell them of Guabancex.
      A goddess whose fury destroys everything.

Juracán, the storm she swirls,
      the word *hurricane,* a bastardized translation—

drifts from one mouth to another.
      Tell them *hurricane* lies arid and unmoving

on the tongue—in bite-sized headlines,
      quick conscientious exchanges on the way to work.

Hurricane sounds like "hurry, cane"
      and sugar boils in the bile and rises

in the throat. Tell them not to speak
      this word. Say, *Juracán.* Let it thrash your mouth

open, shriek it like a prayer,
        sing it like a *son*. Our bodies are potholed

roads of chaos. Sweat tendrils
        down our spine. The way we dance, the whirl

in our walk. The way our desire
        spirals, how we coil and curl—thrust

forward, when touching,
        how we breathe up storms.

Acoustics

All night we craved the touch
      of vine-grappling voice, a drum
down river, clapping
      to cucubano's flutter, a response
to our own bellow. We were unsure
      of everything. At times, even each other.
The hurricane blew out our lights
      in a single exhale—the archipelago
mere wisps of smoke. Our sole
      certainty, abandonment. When all you hear
is darkness, it's easy to disappear.
      Plucked strings and banging on goat
skin, throats sung to callus,
      pockets of people stirring up sound
thundered us alive. Unburying hymns
      from the rubble, lips wet with tremor
and silt, we stood at the beating
      wave, wove a net of vibrating song
from silhouette to silhouette,
      built a lighthouse of our existence.
Years ago, you'd get arrested—
      killed, even—for whistling a revolutionary
tune. Still we whistled. Still we
      whistle, despite imperial boot, gag law
and oblivion. Pulsating our
      presence under a slashed sky.

D.A. interview

Eso nunca se había inundado, y nos sentíamos más seguras,
pero como a eso de las 10:00 a.m. cayó una peña de esas
grandes y bajó todo eso por ahí y le dio un cantazo
a la ventana, y ahí yo no se más
porque la puerta se cerró.

Hilda Gloria González Collazo

I was looking for the portable radio señor oficial   we wanted to listen to
the news   everything outside was shadow   Then the bedroom door
slammed shut on its own   almost kicked off   its hinges like a raging horse
This island has seen hauntings before   trees have gone shy   and water
doesn't stay its course anymore   but I swear even the house shivered   when
that door   closed shut and I lost sight of my sisters   You know how they
say   when one door closes another opens   I think they forgot windows
señor oficial   because that's how it broke in   devoured through that duct-
taped pane   like a pack of strays   howling and scratching   Have you ever
heard landscape avalanche   down a throat   Twigs like nails on a back
clawing at the flesh on the way down   the nasal cavities can't handle
that kind of pressure blasting   cartilage to dust   that you señor oficial
are standing on   a detonation blowing cracks down   the walls down my
bones too   fissures that tug at my insides   when I sit on what's left of my
porch or   bend over   to pick up a piece   of some neighbor's roof   I tried
calling out   to my sisters   but I could hear them   not breathing   makes
you forget to breathe too   you choke on the air   you're trying to swallow
and realize   your sisters in there are teeming   to the teeth   with montaña

almost mountains themselves   I couldn't save them   señor oficial   that
eye was still over us   I was on my knees   so it would look away   but
María summoned   what our walls couldn't handle   what my windows
failed   to hold back

Breath

*After hurricane María, many elderly and bedridden people
dependant on oxygen concentrators died as a result of extended
power outages and/or oxygen depletion. Many of these
were not included in the official, government-issued
death count. Their stories and lives were erased.*

all I can think of is the wind
and how I want it inside me
rolled up in a tobacco leaf / long drag
a smoldering cigar of air filling my

lungs struggle to rise / like unleavened loaves
gasping for the tempest outside
the stillness / in my chest
a field of burnt sugarcane

I watch the light bulb above me
wonder how light flees
glass without shattering
I hear thrashing beyond

the sealed window / whirs of wasted gusts
lace my fingers / into holy patchwork
pray the wind finds its way in
to think my body capable of collapse

beneath sky's toppling / I clutch
at my breath / turn gray / turn ghost
turn gone / turn the switch on
for the love of god / turn on

How to get signal

1. Line up outside the only surviving AM station behind 100 others. 2. Feel your body close to crumpling. It's the fourth line you've been in today. First for water, second for fuel, third for a bag of rice and can of beans. 3. Curl inwards like morivíví, under the scorching sun. Skin dried orange peel, wind gone with the hurricane. 4. Dance the mosquito merengue, with flailing arms and legs. 5. Be careful crossing the copper-cabled river, climbing the hill of debris. 6. Preserve every drop of your water bottle if you have one, they are quickly unbecoming. 7. Think obsessively about your mother who lives two hours away in Arecibo. Wonder if she trimmed the overgrown meaito. 8. Remember your lover lives by El Río Grande de Añasco. That it swells like your breasts when you touch, that it has claimed bodies before. 9. Listen to the whispers and empty-handed prayers before and behind you. You're not the only victim of uncertainty. 10. After hours in line, finally reach your turn on the air, and feel the wind knocked out of you like a projectile launched at your stomach at 155 mph. 11. Lose composure and watch your body turn earthquake. Your shoulders a plunging building, your eyes a tsunami. 12. Listen to the crackling radio waves crash on the shore of your uncontrollable sobbing. 13. Forget everything you wanted to say and just manage *I love you Te amo I love you Te amo I love you Te amo I love you Te amo.* 14. Hope your tears make it across the archipelago, perhaps across the Atlantic. 15. Hope Mr. Jones Act doesn't charge your sorrow a tariff because it sails on a foreign vessel. Tell him you've been trapped on a U.S. shipwreck for 120 years. 16. Hope your love doesn't spoil inside a barge on a dock, hope it's distributed in time. 17. Wipe your eyes, blow your nose, step back outside into the sun and come out to a sea of faces expectantly waiting for their turn.

Backyard burial

We're finding dead people, people who have
been buried, [people] have made common graves [. . .]
We've been told people have buried their family members
because they're in places that have yet to be reached.

Health Secretary Rafael Rodríguez-Mercado

dandelions sprouted from the splitting skin
on the tip of her toes. the grime snug
between flesh and nail when I realized

no one was coming. five days had passed
and my mother, an oxygen-masked ghost
at the flickering menace of a bulb,

grew garden-bed of clover. no wailing
sirens curled up the mountain. only wailing.
no machete-wielding rescue team. only my desperate

swings to clear a patch of welcoming ground.
no emergency funeral procession. only candles
to drag her mossing through humid darkness.

no relief helicopters on my driveway

or tarpless roof. only overhead, like vultures
circling the dying with no promise of swoop,

devouring release. I dug a hole in the backyard
next to the flattened chicken coop. smell of damp
rotting and excrement. cleared slabs of zinc, branches,

vine-choked fence. and waited. for a voice, a footstep,
the slam of a car door. instead, the dull thump
of my mother's body on hollowed wet earth.

Teté: A Tale of Abandonment

"Whoever needs the help, we have to help, [. . .]
Porque son mi gente. Because they are my people.
It got so dark in there when I would go in
that people would say that I was dead.
There are still people today who think that I am dead."

Ernesto "Teté" Matos Santana

I.

Teté is a man of water.
A fisherman from the coast
of Toa Baja. Seventy-nine years
a vessel, combing
through the tendrils
of the Atlantic.

The ocean has been neither
mystery nor fright.
He's done all but sleep
on the seabed—
his hands, boulders
worn by lapping,
open deep.

He's seen the blue's volatile
churn, been through the worst
storms, electric showers—
his body floating
next to his boat to avoid
being struck by lightning.

II.

What of an ocean whose tongue
slips beyond shoreline's bite?

What of water that breaks
outside its terracotta cradle?

What of a hurricane that renounces
the edges of trusted geography?

A fisherman can chart new expanses,
navigate miles through fragile stillness.

But when water is up to your midriff,
the only ridge in sight,

when a school of fish is an actual school,
when your town is submerged

in wildness—this new stretch
of world makes even the bravest

shudder—ripples
untraversable.

III.

No police or uniforms
in sight. No sirens, no
flooding blue and red
lights—only flooding.
No mayor nor helicopters
nor rescue crews. No FEMA
teams or parachutes,
even light fled homes—
was deserting the sky
too. And water
couldn't help
but be
water.

IV.

Teté, fingers cut
by tempest wind, slipped
into his boat and began rowing—
along the newly risen
canals, atop the waterline,

under which creatures
came to life: powerlines,
seething electric eels.
Transformers, gliding manta rays.
Windshield shards, lurking sea

urchins. Teté's life was a spiral
existence—winding lines day in
and day out. Weaving the net
of his life as generously as he could.
Returning, always returning,
to the ocean. Master of the rod,
he reeled in fish unabatedly.

But to reel in people—families
gathered on remaining patches
of tile, folks huddled
on evaporating dryness—
was the first terror
of water he'd held.

V.

His boat could handle five to six
      at once. He was careful to strike

oar to surface,
      to not tip over

the shivering survivors.
      Cutting through sharp

air, the liquid
      of people's lives,

he delivered them
      onto the nearby highway,

where the flood
      was only waist deep.

He rescued fifteen families,
      and every time Teté whorled

back, they would watch
      him melt into the sinking

that befell
      his town—many claiming

they never saw him return.
      It took sixty hours for that body

of water to recede.
      It took months for Tete's body

to recover, reappear.
      Fishing wouldn't call to fishermen

for a great while.
      The bottom of the ocean

saw its own hurricane too.
      Even when Teté heard

the sea's summon,
      he went no further

than the shore.
      Not for a long time.

VI.

Yes—Teté is a man of water.
As fluid and free as possible
in a forgotten colony. But water,
or rather, the abandonment that follows,
can make a tremble of a man.

Scarred As Islands

Noche de San Juan

I left Puerto Rico
on a Noche de San Juan.

By left I mean howled
out the airplane window

the way sirens and strays
put us to sleep each night.

Tradition dictates at midnight
you must fall back into the sea

at least three times to ensure
good fortune all year.

I watched from my window
in Luquillo, bags packed,

as bodies axed through brine,
snapping like tree trunks.

Marveled at the trust
in water. In night and falling

into it. The belief in magic
and some strange providence—

how it might conjure up
an insurrection, vanish

the whole of government, undo
the curse of colonialism.

Plunging one, two, three,
four times into oncoming

waves, a fifth just in case,
hoping that harpooning

yourself into ocean
will change things.

This was how I'd last see the island:
slicing through the deep, looking

to fish out a bottle cap
of sustenance, revolt.

This was how I'd leave:
knowing things wouldn't change—

or worse: they would change
without me. Everyone fell

backwards into the lap
of the Atlantic or Caribbean.

I boarded an overnight flight. My back
shuddering, dry, unblessed by water.

Home

after Safiya Sinclair's "Home"

have I forgotten it—wild conch shell dialect / captive

consonants caved beneath my tongue / our words

from the same backbone / *respirar* and *espiral* / our breath

of cyclical measures / to breathe here—exhales flat

as fog / I practice sighing spirals / fear not breathing

up storms / return is too jagged / a shard / my soles

have pinkened and grown cays / scarred as islands / I swallow

sea glass / hope the waters / will tumble and roll me a

shore lined in bay grape and Indian-almond / lips plump

with guinep—I've sucked on its patience / savored

floating halos of seaweed / eaten fistfuls of sand

the slow-borne sadness / of island and exile / and here I stand

Still / at the edge of this mouth / this insatiable country

in weep and rage and plight / wondering if betrayal

is happiness / in a place not home / forgive this grieving

body / remind it of laughter / roaring / libre / like waves

sloshing lilt / of churned seafoam / of the sea

that again and again / I pray / does not forget my name

Sermon on NYC subway

lights flicker / fireflies / in the stitches of / this city / has yet to fear glass
bulbs hang hushed from half-houses / and crumbling ceilings on my
archipelago / no one asks for light anymore / we've learned to suck on and
savor / the dim brittle—like sacramental / crumbs sift / through our fingers
biblical dust / only the waters rise and grow warm / like fresh loaves—

*people turn to god / when things go wrong / call on him / in times of trouble / but
god is / always here / and when the earth starts shaking / there's not one soul
that's going to stand / not one—*

we call on god / in our goodbyes   *adiós* / name children after him   *Jesús*
suspended from necks / pendulums / of piety / carry the weight of
him   *amén*—why does the earth tremble / beneath us when every day
like sacks full of sand / we spill / onto this earth with his name
blighted bark / in our mouths?

Ode to my studio apartment in Forest Hill, Newark

after Aracelis Girmay

I once read in a poem that there's such a thing
      as the kindness of windows. It's winter—branches chatter
like a fever, and I've never known trees
      to willingly surrender their foliage. I watch the world
from this snowglobe, your scratched glass,
      smudge the surface, patiently wait for late morning.
When the sun comes in through
      your eastern windows, I pull up the venetian
blinds—pull off my clothes, lie—back bare,
      on your wood-checkered floor, tits in the air, a river
of sunlight pouring in. Even though the sun
      behaves differently here, doesn't touch with the tenderness
of my island, your windows do me this kindness,
      and we cheat the cold. I was told I'd be swallowed up
by weather, wouldn't survive the chill
      of this country—its biting ways. But you give me
these moments, delicious heat, hide
      my nakedness even with the blinds up, windows open;
allow me this traveling back, this pleasure
      of winning, of fuck-you to this cold cold place
while my belly hangs cliffside, ribs blossoming
      bougainvillea in the paned warmth, and February
roars outside. You, dearest of square footages,

hold me between your gypsum arms—cries puddling
in my navel, even as I miss and love another
while inside you.

Ladybugs

The house is strewn with them.
Dead. Their dotted mounds

mountain from every which corner
and surface of the former school

turned short-term rental in Hancock, NY.
Someone mentions climate change.

Others say they only live for a year.
We have yet to come across a ladybug

crawling. I spot one in the shower—
six legs upturned, rocking like a raft

against the downpour, slowly
ushered by water towards the whirl.

Meanwhile, Ecuador nurses
a tidal uprising against a neoliberal state.

The Kurds fight off swells
of Turkish armies and US intervention.

Periodically, ladybugs wash up
on shores in masses, like seaweed.

Only a few survive the crossing
in their mysterious plunge.

Back home in Puerto Rico, pensioners
crash pots outside mansions of members

of la Junta, and island municipalities halt
water transit, teaching public officials

lessons on abandonment.
Suds gather around my toes

like barnacles as I lather my feet.
The leaves outside obey

the fiat of Fall, and it all goes back to water.
These days, it seems, no matter where you are,

there's always something or someone swimming
against it, trying to make it to shore, drowning—

relinquishing a fighting chance
to the insistent swirl of drain.

Another ladybug surges downstream,
tickles my skin with its strokes,

frantically trying to avoid
the tug, the silver edge.

Shutters

Somewhere in upstate New York,
where everything is monochrome,

balding, I press my forehead
against the Greyhound window.

My body hurts today. A fever swells
in my joints, surges into the narrow

canal between bone and tissue.
This is not the heat I lust for in front

of snow-freckled glass. The bus passes
haunting victorians, their wood struck shy

by weather, barns stretchmarked
with age. They all reflect my gaze, shutters

fluttering lashes against the gale.
Quaintly tacked to prim facades.

Heat boils inside my wrists, shoulders.
In my archipelago, shutters don't adorn

a house's high relief. Are not ornament
of choice—but armor, protection against a storm,

a permanent doing. As I fever
through this country, I hear

hammering split the streets of Puerto Rico.
Hundreds of public schools—shuttered.

Foreclosed homes—shuttered. Bakeries,
hairdressers, pharmacies—shuttered.

Clinics—shuttered. Pensions—shuttered.
Campuses—shuttered. Rivers, coastlines,

and acres—shuttered. I traverse
a graying expanse, my chest a bonfire.

I take a pill to shutter this body.
There are hours left to this ride.

GERD

I told her there was a sea urchin
lodged in my throat. My last days
on the archipelago, I drank up
ocean tendrils— it must've swirled
in, nestled in tissue reef. The
doctor asked if Puerto Rico was
ready to receive tourists. *Is it back
in shape after the hurricane?* I told
her tourists have been breaking in
since 1493. Puerto Rico was never
ready. Never willing. She placed
her fingers on my throat. Slid
them up and down its length like
a ghost crab. Asked me to open
my mouth, dangled a lighthouse,
a fishing rod, inside of me. *You
have GERD.* Anxiety-induced. She
wants to vacation in the Caribbean
with her husband. Her hand on my
jaw, otoscope hooked on my parted
lips—open as a littoral cave; I
caught a reflection in her eyes—an
island, docked at the bottom of my
swallow. She shone the light deeper,
down where this chip of sand clung
to flesh; probed my body to cough

it up. She prescribed Prevacid for a month. To coat my stomach from the violence sloshing, stop the surge up my throat—the singe of leaving this island I carry at the root of every breath.

Leaving

Como la isla
caimos todxs en desuso
mirando desde la ventanita del avión
el sueño del retorno haciéndose pequeño
apenas una hormiga en la mirada
alzando vuelo
sin saber a donde.

Nicole Cecilia Delgado

In Puerto Rico, overnight flights
from Aguadilla, sometimes San Juan,
to who knows where, are a staple
of revolving door migration—revolver
Russian roulette. They are the cheapest
runway departure, the cheapest run-away
from this sutured raft adrift at sea.

It also makes it easier to leave. The night.
You can't see what the turbine shreds
behind you, abandons below.

Darkness teethes around the brush
and your parents' house beneath it.
The acerola and pana pepita tree.
The side of the road where Ernesto

stands, trunk choked with quenepa.
The road that leads up to country, ankles
prickly with cadillo, chicharras tuning their legs.
The tuna factory that apologizes to the bay.
The bay that stills at the apology. The chinchorro
on stilts, coconut and cinnamon chichaito, what remains
of your friends and their last drink before morning.

From the airplane window,
it looks like you're only leaving
a blotch of sea. (Power goes out
so often in Puerto Rico. Your parents
are without electricity since yesterday
afternoon.) You can't trust evening lights
to guide you back home, convince you
otherwise, ask you to stay.

This is the flying the expelled
can barely afford, a shadowed
leaving—thickened by Saharan dust.

Fucking lies if airlines say they don't know
what they're doing, if the government
gasps its foul mouth open,
when they lower ticket prices,
trip the breaker, unplug
the archipelago.

Educación

after Lark Omura

Always swim towards an oncoming wave, then dive.

Never swim against the current, let it hurl you out to sea, then wade back ashore.

The shore is lined with sargassum and sea grape, not littered.

Don't litter the sand that straddles a Leatherback's young.

Leatherbacks leave for ocean and migrate years before returning.

Returning will die on the airport runway, buried inside your rib cage.

Your rib cage will resprout with return through graveyard soil.

Keep mice away from the soil you pile into pots of ají and white basil.

A good pot of white rice colors your lips with oil.

Pour oil into the pot to pave it with pegao.

Don't throw away pegao, the scraping hides resistance.

Cats will hide hours before a hurricane.

The eye of a hurricane opens the eyes of a people.

The eyes of a people can grow clouded with Saharan dust.

Saharan dust crosses the Atlantic, storms through windows of foreclosed homes.

To occupy a foreclosed building is to step on a police anthill.

The police will tear gas you because you fight for education.

The police will tear gas you because you fight.

The police will tear gas you.

Tear gas washes off with vegetable oil, water, and Palmolive.

Watch water at your ankles, it could be raining upriver.

El Río Guanajibo, el Río Mameyes will bathe you when your pipes and faucet parch.

When you're parched for day's end, have a Medalla.

A Medalla won't raise your salary or free Puerto Rico, but tonight, it'll do.

Tonight, listen for the strange music of sirens and chicharras.

Tonight, imagine sirens lure to shipwreck away from your archipelago.

Tonight, let news of your archipelago watch itself.

Instead, watch for Dominicana and the Virgin Islands watching you, just as eager for your hand.

Tonight, when the power goes out, give your neighbor a hand—connect them to your generator.

Tonight, connect last year's Christmas lights and count all the burnt-out bulbs.

Tonight, from New Jersey, count the days till you come back home.

Only the Ocean Answers

Reservoir

I've tried connecting a hose to
my tear ducts, but my grief, the
men in uniform tell me, is not
potable. I must wait for bottles
to rain from the sky. I must wait
for aisles to be restocked. I must
wait for truckloads of aseptic
charity. I must wait. I must wait.
To die. With dry tongues at the
sweat on my thighs. Not even a
flowerpot to bury me. Which is
why I've been crying into milk
gallons. A faucet leaking moisture
and misery down throats that
have known of the first, too little,
of the second, too much. With
long guns and shaded eyes, from
the perimeters of their fortress,
always a rifle's distance away—the
men in uniform fear my reservoir
of sorrow will drown them.

Laundry

Resilience lay there.
Reeking in the mountain

of laundry that had been piling up
for weeks, as I waited for my faucet to sputter.

And resilience grows rank with waiting.
So I threw it in a basin with some water

from the river I begged would stay its course,
and washed it. Until it bled red like downhill

gashes. Howled like the haunting
that stranded us. Gasped for air,

pleaded for forgiveness. Wrung it dry
until my bones splintered like the house

next door, where I used to cook and cry
and love. Until it didn't fit anymore. Stretched out.

Unraveling. I clipped it on to the washing
line to dry. Sat down on my wet mattress.

Watched it hang limp—battered
by sun-tinged winds. A tattered rag.

To love an island

is lips / between legs / crunch of sand
under your tongue / in the hollow / between teeth

is salty dew / beneath sheets / above the lip
seaweed silhouette / of your body

is blue tarps / over your fucking
mosquitoes / lodged behind your knees

is candlelight / wax intimacy / and blister / the stamina
of a switch / short-circuits / under your thrusting / hurricane

is sooted brush of mouths / dust down your rivered
throat / to your Superfund / womb

is anchors / from US boats / run by a US crew / with a US flag
built in a US shipyard / fastened to keep from drifting
from being island / the patchwork of decades-old wounds
sewn shut with twigs / and coconut fiber

is 2 AM deep / in night terrors / blotting sweat and pus
tissues rank with / disaster / a kiss on the forehead / every evening

is a growing distance / a foot caught / in barbed wire
PROPIEDAD PRIVADA / on your bedroom door

is leaving

is never learning / how to swim
knowing / that it ends / with drowning

American Airlines Flight #188

To Julia Keleher, Puerto Rico's (ex) Secretary of Education,
who was on the same American Airlines flight as I was
four months after Hurricane María

you probably think 188 is not a big number
you paid five times that figure for your priority seat
your annual salary was 1,330 times higher
and they're only schools, there are more, seven flattened towns over

you probably haven't realized this is a full flight
that a percentage of more than 25,000 students
that left the schools you closed are passengers

but i'm no statistician
the count is constantly changing
and i'm losing my breath

you probably think the steady rumble growing beneath you
is the plane's engine or new massage technology
it doesn't cross your mind that you're sitting atop
the belly of this american air-beast
digesting the crumbs of forced flight

the plane is trying to take off, spitting, coughing up fuel
while you breathe easy, even this monster heaves under
the human weight on its titanium back

is a direction you've never looked to before—
that sea of blue fema tarps
rolling green military trucks
golden sands of schools' remains
a paradise of your making

trimming the bushes, the bougainvillea, the budgets
you fly willingly, with priority promise of return
and slingshot numbers, pout to piña colada
from a roofed-over patio table in your backyard

Newspaper interview

No es fácil perder a tres hermanas juntas.
Casi toda la familia ... Vivieron juntas toda la vida
y siempre decían que querían irse juntas.

Wilfredo González Collazo

I'm haunted by the river their house overlooked   río *viví,* river *lived*
The past tense a rusting   fish hook in my throat   They were born like
waves breaking at sea   one right after the other   My sisters never
married   no children   devout christians   Seven decades in each others'
company   that morning   only inches apart under 8 feet of mountain
And it took 8 days to get them out   to open the door to a tightness
not even death could slip into   Soil finds its way   into the slimmest
crevice   of breath   The neighbors complained about the smell
the river *viví* was still swollen   purpled with broken   *Lived,* it licked
its edges   a thick tongue   on fractured lips   Like the river their bodies
a sick circularity   buried to unbury and bury again   Except their
corpses were seized   scrutinized, stuffed with 700 others   tagged
to this day unnamed   We finally saw them again   the 8th of may
8 months after the storm   a numeric uncanniness   Held them   boxes
of ash   returned as mountain   Today the house is hillside   wildness
grown   into devouring thickness   a room of smothering green   halls
trailed with wet earth   all held together by faded yellow tape   *Viví*
surges on days of heavy rainfall   They *lived*   Only ferns and vines
of velvet bean are testament   to the river's hymn

When a tree falls

Ah, what an age it is
When to speak of trees is almost a crime
For it is a kind of silence about injustice!

Bertolt Brecht, *To Posterity*, translated by H. R. Hays

but even the trees speak
snapping like dry bones / under the foot

of weather / slung over sparking
power lines / last attempt at sustained flight

branches a thousand arms / reaching
bark marbled fungus and termite

consider the fright of a flamboyán / skirt upturned
robbed of red / roots ripped / from earth's scalp

consider the cry of a carambola / struck down
putrid sweet on ground / lost aspiring body of the cosmos

consider the plight of a plantain / self-suffocated
wrapped in its own leaf / hijos dying inside

sprouting back like jagged teeth / twisting arthritic fingers
to not speak of trees / is a kind of silence about injustice

for when a tree falls in an archipelago / and the world
is around to hear it / the tree is no longer a tree

semantics like leaves change / memory rooted into body
seven months piled on a sidewalk / blocking the ſtreet

at your doorſtep / blighted wood and abandonment
death at its sloweſt / an unblinking mirror

ſteadfaſt ruſtle / if a people fall
in an archipelago / and the world hears it

only the ocean / responds
with a swallow

Rhizomatic

*By Porto Rican law the entire beach of the island is government property,
for sixty feet back of the water's edge. As a consequence, what would
in our own land be the choicest residential section is everywhere
covered with squatters, who pay no rent, and patch their miserable
little shelters together out of tin cans, old boxes, bits of driftwood,
and yagua or palm-leaves, the interior walls covered, if at all,
with picked-up labels and illustrated newspapers.*

Harry A. Franck, *Roaming Through the West Indies*, 1920

Mangroves now lie on the side
of the road. Cut and left

on the dirt path leading to the bay,
where people from the capital,

or from the continent, have been
building second or third homes.

As if the waterfront wasn't home
already. Long ago, times only the salt

can claim, these edges of land
were shunned, deemed disease-ridden,

too poor to inhabit, too precarious
a stretch of marginal acreage.

A blue expanse was anything but useful,
laden with reef and memory.

But their story lies here. In water.
The one constant, always calling.

There were many names for them, you see.
Squatters, informal dwellers, deedless

in square-footage. But these coasts have long
known their footfall, sand swallowed

their prints and their ancestors',
soil seen the growth and harvest of cane

and their children. Like mangroves,
their existence is intertidal—

led by the comings and goings
of blue, brine and resolute rooting.

Their fingers are tattooed with clasp
of land crab, prying of clams and oysters,

nibble of fish and estuary waters,
sharp imprecision of machete on coconut.

This land is no one's. This land is of itself.
But it took them in. Made a home

of them in return. So they too taste
the pierce, the bleeding fence—

acid whispers of *private* and *profit*.
They're wanted gone. Offered to repair

their homes after the storm, if only they move
inland—recede, swell-like, from the shore.

Let another hurricane come.
They grow rhizomatic on this saline earth.

Breaking news

Small cargo ship intercepted 120 miles
out at sea US military deployed
plantains on board handcuffed
and questioned Attempts to appeal futile
caught green-handed trying to enter
without corresponding permits
Deportation to Dominican Republic
expected after further questioning
by Department of Homeland Security

*

Government of Puerto Rico welcomes
benevolent capitalists looking for tax
haven to establish crypto-colony
Department of Economic Development
and Commerce devises blueprints
for first cryptocurrency bank
Discussions on Puertopian citizenship
take place in Congress Bitcoin miners
concerned over extended power outages
Organized prayer circles led around
Ceiba trees No comment from locals
profound frustration over plantain shortage

Late in the evening

puerto rico prende sus luciérnagas
para aparecer:
luz ansiosa en el mapamundi.
      //
puerto rico turns on its fireflies
in order to appear:
an anxious light on the world map.

Raquel Salas Rivera

from the eastern tip of Dominicana,
they say you can see Puerto Rico
flutter,

lone firefly in the dark.
late in the evening, across 237 miles of sea,
and then some more, this flicker, wavering

candle wick, floating
ceremony of slow death
is too often sole reminder of our birth

mark on this planet—a wave
to the world, satellites above, incalculable immensity
of space. whereas in any other instance, cartography,

with its fat thumb, would stir us
into the waters. but, late in the evenings,
we are picture-framed firework

of imported fossil fuel,
hanging from earth's
dark canvas. late one evening,

from the eastern tip of Dominicana,
they say they saw a splash, a sputter—
a hand coming down like a sinking

ship, fingers wet and eager
to meet at the flame.
and they wondered about mouths,

which was bigger, the night sky
or the ocean. the slicker throat.
to have gobbled up light,

not even a shadow of archipelago
remaining. no one else wondered
about the stretch of bright that sunk

like a pebble. bulbs are easily replaced,
a blown fuse tossed—why else are waters
as deep as they are if not to submerge

the forgotten. only those
on the eastern tip
of Dominicana lit candles,

late in the evening, set them afloat,
and released jars of restless
fireflies into the night.

Forced Flowering

Sargassum

There's so much   to be learned   from that which floats   A patience
    from the Gulf of Mexico   to a sea of its name   sargassum
drifts hand in hand   with itself   across moleculed drowning   Ripples orange
    then brown   ocean vine climbing   buoyant for sunlight
This algae moves   as model islands   nursing its dwellers   pipefish crabs
    and nudibranch   protecting its young   flailing turtles   sovereign
from the tips of leaves   to the swell   and safety   of crawlers and hidden
    Salt shrub archipelago   breeds by fracture   but never behaves as such
always watching   for myths   of dry land   and the men   who wet for it
    like Columbus   spearing his foot   to find it unfirm   unconquerable
yet he is not the invasion   Blamed the brined bush   on his shoe   for a bloom
    no longer bound   by spiraling currents   Now swims
in factory and filth   burning waters   is wrung to birth   and birth
    itself onto shores   where cruises worry to suffer   this forced flowering
let them suffer   this flowering   Remind us   to survive the surge
    self-suffice   sail the uprise   to be islands   teach us
to stay afloat   to flee   the sinking

Tulips

Tulips sprouted
the first crash.

Blown in from Istanbul
to River Scheldt, never before seen,

this shy-petaled bulb drove the Dutch
delirious. They fertilized prices

and promised tulips, and those tulips' children,
and the children of their children, to moneyed

men—trading in the wind.
This 17th century wildness

flowered a crash that bruised the early buds
of capitalism. I bus to the nearest ShopRite

and buy a bouquet. Stuff stems
in a vase, place it at table's center,

feel nearer the equator
for a shift in the world.

Tulips are not of the tropics.
Neither are banks or the debt they drilled

in my island, their mouths at the puckered
hole. Imagine their throats crammed yellow

and pink. Tulips tearing down
the Spanish forts gnawing our coastlines,

planted in their stead, sowing the safety
their violence kept at bay. The gold ships sailed on,

hounded—tore through blue
tissue for, gold of rivered murders,

lashed from backs, gold
on dirt teeth, pecked

by vultures—all ground
to compost for the tulips lining

our shores. Tulips glutting engines
of seafront military bases,

sinking cruises, smothering
18-holed resorts, the potholed

roads leading to them. Downpouring
on charter schools and for-profit colleges,

seeping through roofs. Rooting cracks
into prisons and police stations.

Strewn down aisles, tiling Walmart
floors. To dream in tulips.

The ShopRite blossoms
wither in a week's passing,

petals never fully fanned.
The vase sits empty of their muck,

earth worming
down the drain.

Clementines

after Mario Benedetti

I pick two from the low-lying
crisper drawers of my fridge.
     Day mists through the window

     like citrus drizzle, as if the sun
were also thumbed through,
     peeled. It's almost November again—

     clementine season.
But honey lingers
     on morning light,

     and leaves refuse the wardrobe
change, dangerous
     uncertainty of weather.

     I sit on the couch and open
Benedetti's poem, "Gajos."
     It helps to think of the heart

     as a clementine. Of its shape
as torn into wedges.
     Only one remaining

faithful to the body
that ripens. He says
       of the heart that while all

       the other gajos suffer,
flee, there is one
       that endures, stays

       for the panic. The balming.
The recovery while ribs
       slacken their grip. I send the poem

       to my father back home
in Puerto Rico, as I've grown
       accustomed to sharing my feelings

       with him through strangers'
words. He responds
       that the poem is beautiful.

       And the three-dotted snake
of his typing reappears.
       ¿Tú tienes ese gajo aún?

       I feel for the rinds perched
on the couch beside me.
       He knows this question

probes a field
long fallow. I leave
        the message seen

        and unanswered—
place another sliver
        in my mouth.

Common reed

When I ride the train into Manhattan
I often realize I care little for going

to the city—it's the idea I thrill
for. Watching the skyline swell

like a dried mushroom
against the boiling blue.

And then I learn
this is not what I ride for

either. It's the common reed.
How it stirs silver in autumn

sun, wilds in
the wetland quiet.

How it tells me something
about myself. The sadness

that squeals from the tired tracks.
No—that rises like steam, seeps

into my marrow. The sadness that is my
sadness—sprouting in stalks from my body

between the cityscapes. To quiver freely
against machine and gale, to sigh

itself inside me, and watch
the train slice by.

Self-portrait as brown pelican

I trust the water, but not

the bird that spreads

like oil spill across

this blue wavering.

I arrow through

seventy feet of air,

plunge-dive

into myself. Break

the ripple of noon

sun with my beak,

never let it clot

to scar. The

pouch in my throat

sloshes with pincers

that scissored off a part

of me, salt-singed

with every cancer

I've scooped up, swallowed,

from these Caribbean

coordinates. This archipelago's coast

no longer feeds me. I burrow

into my own feathers

for sustenance, some kind

of shelled hope.

There's no flying away

from this mangrove

nest—no longer

a colony of my kind,

just a colony—

even though the sky

unfurls into more

sky, casts off clouds

into something other

than this ache

encircled by water.

So I will stay here,

a harpoon splintering

ocean's pane, until I blind,

and hear the seabed,

the land that labors

above it, this winged self,

loved to wholeness again.

Cracked

I leapt from one island to the next   like a child
hop ing   for soft landing
                                       ravaging
                sadness   like a
papaya
      The hurricane left   nakedness   blew

          open   mouths
            kissing the fall   of

    sky—cracked   like   that island
too familiar to   myself
                             the way of return

               required   closing   gapes
   I   so painfully open

Guillotine—A Flag

Forgive me when I speak of land

Forgive me if when I speak
of myself, I speak of land.

If the mountain of my name
earthfalls at the question.

If to the question's insistence,
my response boards a boat

and travels south.
If in this traveling south,

you are disappointed
by the distance, my wavering

silhouette. If the distance returns
me to island—if at *island*,

I ask you to dock in the harbor
between the first two letters. If in this

docking, I ask you to look at
the   *I*   from overhead, the way you

would look at fish. Look
at how it floats on the white

of the page, waterlocked.
If the eye waterlocks

in the looking. If in the looking,
I ask if *I* is not island? If *I* am

not island? If after asking,
I tell you I'm invoked

by the word, the tender lean
of the letter into adjacent topography,

its intimate shrouding,
touching strip of soil.

If the intimate conceivement
of self is to call upon a history

of place, summon the spirit
of home. If when I write

a poem, every poem I write
is home. If when I write

this poem, I ask you to forgive me
for the earth tumbling out of my mouth.

In the fissures

we live

brewing coffee with soil from the old flower pot
threatening the guanábana tree, the beanstalk, with our gaze
rescuing schools sewn shut with golden thread

from paycheck to paycheck
borrowed embrace to borrowed embrace
fearing it'll prove us debtors
of this raft whistling itself empty

postponing tomorrow, clothes unhung
we've yet to iron and fold, a post-it note
with all the bills we have to pay, waiting
for the kind of breeze that'll rob bulbs of their light

we live
without remedy
without patch and plaster
oftentimes without escape
under the turbine of outbound flights
shredding our ceilings to polyethylene rain

propane nights dancing to AM static
bathing a lover in cupfuls
or waiting for rain

spending the last of your cash
on a round for your comrades
because this too is solidarity

and though many are uncomfortable
with the thought, in the fissures there is joy,
without it, there is death

and sometimes we die by the hand of a husband
and sometimes we die by the hand of the state
and sometimes we die by our own hand

he was jealous
health insurance didn't cover it
the boat didn't set sail towards the main island
endurance collapsed under the light post
that still gashes through our homes

and sometimes the fissure is the Atlantic
sometimes we carry the fissure in our ribs from so much leaving
sometimes it cuts like a finger does the sea

and we love in loseta (not close together,
the way boleros were once danced,
though we love in this way too—
all tight, squished up, atop each other,
because the space is so small,
and our desire so immense),
we're fragmented in our love,

our daily comings and goings, our tired
history, tiling the coastline in this mosaic

this is how we love
this, how we fight
with rain water up to our knees
almost river, always imagining
a new way
out to sea

from these selfsame fissures
so very suffered
but so very ours

Island ghazal

On an island, what makes a prophet?
On an island, who makes a profit?

Tousled mangroves, nimble fingers, net flingers,
land crabs, pry the meat, share the sweet—prophet.

Coastline, sea brine, barbed acre, hand shakers,
construction permit, just drill and burn it—profit.

Rescued school, farmed green, fixed cracks, cooking for forty,
art in hallways, for some a bed, families fed—prophet.

Shuttered school, vine-choked fence, wild grass, hot cement,
broken glass, tied up horse, neighs once, no response—profit.

Intercrop, bean pods, ají dulce, lettuce ponds, eggplant,
worm and ant, smell of earth, soil in birth—prophet.

Monocrop, endless rows, GMOs, climate resistant, capital's insistence,
starbucks, big bucks, on a boat, down your throat—profit.

En capucha, green bandana, purple shirt, rainbow flag, seattle in your bag,
free hair, fist in air, for Puerto Rico you'll dare, anything—prophet.

Baton and bullet, riot shield, tear gas, never yield, blocked street,
wall street, cushioned banks, corporate class, watch the glass—profit.

Barter and trade, self-made currency, solidary economy, barbershops,
pharmacies, restaurants, bakeries, artisans, musicians, poets—prophet.

Cruise ships, crypto dicks, paradise, won't suffice, build a city,
atop the city, of desert reefs and homes—profit.

Cancel the debt, that's not our debt, won't pay the debt, illegal debt,
colonial debt, fuck the debt, no longer afraid of your threat—prophet.

Won't cancel the debt, this is your debt, no receipts, pay the debt, this legal
debt, forever mine debtors, forever yours debt, fear my threat—profit.

They say in their own land, no one is a prophet.
They say on an island, to make a profit, kill a prophet.

A cada lechón le llega su renuncia

after El Verano Boricua 2019

Every Western revolution began
with a beheading, a compa recalls.

The drums perched at the barricades,
in front of the governor's mansion,

beat for nothing less. A roasted pig's
head is passed across the wild grass

of outstretched arms, unwavering
in their demand. Wrapped around

the open snout, a white ribbon, bold
black letters. *A cada lechón le llega su renuncia*.

The rest of the pig's body
is slowly severed to its parts

at a wooden table,
right off the raging halo.

The machete plummets
into meat, nicks the tree

martyred for this moment.
Brittled skin flies on impact,

grease drips down fingers, table's ends.
The drums pick up the pace.

The crowd convulses as the swine
face travels above their heads—

we all want a taste
of fresh cleave.

Ode to the cacerola combativa

Me tienen miedo será,
me tienen miedo será.

Cacerola Girl

Kitchens mourn your betrayal,
passersby fold over their ears.

You came to us south-born,
like the winds, clanging

your call over mountain ranges
to fire, to frontline, to freedom.

You were combative way before
you took to devouring streets.

Feeding peoples off the scrape
of your metal, the burnt flakes

of urgent ladle and boil. From rooftops
and twenty-story buildings, innermost

wild grasses and tarped homes,
you drowned out the evening

sirens and warfare press conferences.
The dents we dealt you bruised

to music, turned ſteelpan,
we played you to arm's knot

and detriment. You—chosen inſtrument
of insurreċtion. Riot police marched

on cobbled ſtreets and you
rang in the realization,

nos tienen miedo será,
nos tienen miedo será...

And so we shed our own fear.
Tear gas hurt nothing like the tear

we drummed through days
of militancy againſt the boys' club

behind barricades, inside
the governor's mansion.

Your cuts peeled back, scorched
leaves. Aluminum—baby ferns

unfurling to early sun.
You, so glorious

against the flames piled up
along streets and storefronts,

throbbing in our hands as we weighed
your transformation into weapon.

Fierísima cacerola, let your mangled
face be remembered as we fight off

the tug to return to this violent
place we call normalcy.

Thrum through lull, play us—
insistent and enraged.

The Governor and the Cock

El deporte de los gallos en Puerto Rico
es altamente regulado por el Gobierno,
es un pilar cultural y representa un
importante sector económico en nuestra Isla.

Tweet by Ricardo Rosselló, (ex)Governor of Puerto Rico

A cis man is willing to go through hardest of lengths for his cock.
The governor is no different. Twenty-four women are dumped at the lip
of some stream, a shaft of bridge. Feminists claw blood from police altars
and sleep on cobblestone. The government whips out its ranks and sprays—
red thins to river. He won't sign their executive order. A hand comes down—
marble fisted—on spurred island cocks. Trainers unzip their mouths, haul
out their cages. A state of emergency is declared. He will fight to protect
their cocks. Bush-born and reared on stroke, their right to brawl is learned.
Blows, an act of cultural preservation. Jabbing, an inherited sport, a cock's
training. He will defend the safety of their violence—plumed quarrels
and thrusts erect to kill. Why change history now? This animal given
nothing to peck but power. And power goes straight to the head.
But the head knows, as the cock crows, and morning is forced out of bed,
that the pit will erode to ruin—the chopping block in its stead.

And sometimes the bullet is cis man

Puerto Rico es una bala hinchada entre mi pecho.
Es algo que me duele, que me seca el retoño.
Por su culpa soy trescientas bombillas
de ilusión apagada...

      /

Puerto Rico is a bullet lodged in my chest.
It's what hurts me, what sucks my spring dry.
Because of Puerto Rico I'm three hundred
light bulbs of illusion gone dead.

Marigloria Palma
translation by Carina del Valle Schorske

And sometimes the bullet is cis man. And sometimes it's machete,
a pocket knife, a bottle, gasoline. To wake up each morning to three hundred
light bulbs of lucha gone dead. It's not enough we lose power on the weekly
at home, but lose our lives too. And the closer to night a woman stands,
the more she's taught to fear it. Puerto Rico, too many macharranes lurk
between the wildness of your legs, sit at the head of your table in bloom.
We're so tired of reading you die in twelve point font and coffee stains—
of the stains bleached out with the scrub brush of the state. Your waters
are warming, our bodies rise with them. Clap cis men on the mouth who lean
left but always think they're right. Fight the right that protects the safety
of their violence. Let their violence tremble walking down the street, we will
no longer. The street is not our foe; our fear—bitter fuel. A fury fueled
by street lamp, a desk, the bed, the stove, a bar, a dance, the frontlines.
The frontlines, picket-fenced with our faces, hands clasped to spark.

A cada lechón le llega su Navidá combativa

after El Verano Boricua 2019

The walls of Old San Juan
are decked with the spirit

of the season: *Navidá Combativa 2019*—
spray-painted in blue, sealed with spit.

These are not Christmas lights
that flutter across storefronts,

balconies overhead. The streets are aflame
again. Our first cleaving still sizzles at the edge

of our mouths—how we watched
his head boulder off a cliff, into the sea.

What a thing to behold, all the while
steadying the compass reeling in our chests.

Our machetes quiver afresh, rods spin
in the ready over the crossfires of this country.

A new pig sits at the head of the hogpen
we've come to call the governor's mansion.

A nation so hungry, a single swine
will not suffice to quell the carnage

we're owed, the debt carved
from us like meat off a bone.

The entire sty is in for a butchering.
A cada lechón le llega su renuncia,

rang through la Calle de la Resistencia,
the newly minted streets of Puerto Rico,

in the summer swelter. Winds cool,
and we labor to guard our flickering rage.

The swells swallow coastlines anew,
breezes stir Caribbean pines.

Christmas is here. And people
know that this time of year

el lechón se coge, se mata y se pela;
se pone en la vara y se le da candela.

Hummingbirds, molotovs and other such things

after Nazim Hikmet

I may never give a speech that will play across the pixel
field of phones—that hummingbirds will carry from
beak to gnarled forest, branching generations.

I may never be the courage whispered into someone's ear
as they cover and crouch in hiding—wet the lips
of the clandestine, the exiled, the fierce at the frontlines.

I may never stare down from a banner, usher miles
of march, masked faces—nor echo through air
with molotovs hurled in my name, blistering streets.

I may not be read in the damp, fog of cigarettes, erotic tug
of liberation—crumpled and pulled out of pockets, sieved
through a megaphone, rallying thousands to flame.

I may not be resurrected every year for encampments at the hill
of my militant legacy. Nor made into page and bound. Debated in circles.
Slipped into budding hands. Invoked by combat. Despised by comfort.

There may be no documentaries. No songs or poems.
Sunflowers, candles, hand-sewn flags. No pamphlets,
postcards, letters, or notes. No reason or necessity, really.

But I will know the beauty of living—dying, in the anonymity
of everything and everyone, the rearguard and collective shadow,
with nothing to show for it, but an archipelago, a world, closer to our imagining.

Let it tremble

We want to speak
of earthquakes, but trip
over our rubbled throats
and say *hurricane* instead.

We found warehouses glutted
with light and expired water,
haven't showered in days
and only have memory
of power walking out
the door, taking the bill with it.

Yet again, the ground trembles.
We haul ourselves to the epicenter
of disaster. Roads jammed with truckloads
of ixora and solidarity, the Three Wise Men
trading camels for cargo beds, birthday candles
blown out at a gas station, the side of the road.

We break like tidal wave
into the warehouses, reclaim
the supplies as our own.
Take helplessness, the bile
of our daily burden, digest it
and whistle out hummingbirds.

Stuff ourselves back
into La Calle de la Resistencia,
swap flag for guillotine, parade it
through tear-gassed air. Sound pots
and pans from twenty-first floors.
Rebaptize streets. Suffocate highways.
Fissure verse onto walls. Launch cobblestones
like comets. Howl to live drum. Pulverize glass
to sugar. Grind up on each other combatively.

We don't know each other
but distribute tenderness
with organizational urgency.
Sew mosquito nets in heaps, hopes.
Set up traveling showers, circuses
of laundry machines. Cook for entire
neighborhoods. Hold each other when
night's curtain falls, still submerged
in darkness. Tighten our embrace
when it trembles once again.

And let it tremble. Let them tremble.
Our murderers. The colonizers and their colonized.
The whole blood-marbled edifice. For we've swallowed
it all—hurricanes, earthquakes, meteorites, debt,
invasions, and fear with our morning coffee.

The streets—ours. The shriveled rivers,
the eroded coasts, the ashen plains,
the superfund flowers, the shuttered

corner stores, the basketball courts
without hoops, the carcassed public
plazas, the accordion schools, the hospitals
without power—the hospital laid
brick by brick—the poisoned town
halls, the foreclosed homes, the ruin,
all ours. Puerto Rico is ours. Even if it
trembles again and collapses atop us entirely.

Smallness

How odd it is, then, an oddness that doesn't escape
a single writer from an island country,
that we have to return to our small islands,
if only to remember how to live large.

Marlon James, *So Many Islands*

no le debemos a nadie la pequeñez.
            /
we owe no one smallness.

Raquel Salas Rivera, *la independencia (de puerto rico)*

I stand on a mountain in Ponce,
high up as I've ever been.
See the land descend onto itself,

untie its locks into a tangle
of green. The wind brushes
through banana leaves

and ixora shrubs, African tulip trees
and breadnut, combing the long mane
curling out to sea. My breathing opens

with the altitude, enormity
fruiting softly down
to island's edge.

An entire world sprawls
beneath. If I reach far enough
into the soil that steadies

my feet, I'll find threshed
words decomposing
near the bedrock.

Shells of *isolated,* once *insulatus,* as in,
"made into an island." Pods of *insular,*
once *insularis,* meaning, "narrow, isolated."

How we've been made to feel minute.
How our geography has been wielded
against us, corralled in by dimension.

I crumble the earth in my hands.
Grind the old, dried husks
to rain between my fingers.

There's a largeness to breath in Puerto Rico,
a freedom that follows. Spread wide
as the bush and valleys below me.

Notes

"A hurricane has come and gone. What do we tell our children now?": 1) The title of this poem was borrowed from the article "Coping with Post-Hurricane Psychologically: A Parent's Perspective" by Keiya George, published in *VI Life and Style Magazine*. **2)** Part of the poem was informed by "Fin a un mito: la deidad taína de los huracanes se llama Guabancex, no Juracán" by *Primera Hora*; the entry "La tríada: Guabancex - Coatrisquie - Guataubá" from *Pueblos Originarios: Dioses y Personajes Míticos*; and the *Wikipedia* entries "Juracán" and "Guabancex."

"D.A. interview": The poem's epigraph is a quote from the article "Mueren tres hermanas por derrumbe en Utuado tras paso de María" by Femmy Irizarry Álvarez, published in *Primera Hora*.

"How to get signal": 1) Right after Hurricane María's passing over Puerto Rico, telecommunication systems were down for weeks. For the first few weeks after the hurricane, a handful of AM radio stations throughout the entire archipelago were the only available and functioning means of communication. People started going to these radio stations to try to let their loved ones know how they were and find out about their state and well-being. **2)** The Jones Act, or the Merchant Marine Act of 1920, requires all goods shipped between U.S. ports to be transported by U.S. vessels built on such soil and operated by Americans.

"Backyard burial": The poem's epigraph is a quote from the article "Hurricane Maria's death toll in Puerto Rico is higher than official count, experts say" by Omaya Sosa Pascual, published in *Miami Herald*.

"Teté: A Tale of Abandonment": This poem borrows from, was aided and informed by the piece "Maria's Bodies" by Mattathias Schwartz, published in *New York Magazine*. The poem's epigraph is a quote from this piece as well.

"Home": The line "have I forgotten it—wild conch-shell dialect" was borrowed from Safiya Sinclair's "Home," as was "of the sea that again and again I pray does not forget my name," but the latter underwent slight modifications.

"American Airlines Flight #188": The number of schools in the poem (188) combines the alleged number of public schools closed by Julia Keleher and the government pre–Hurricane María and post–Hurricane María at the time the poem was written. However, it's important to mention that accurate government-issued statistics and documentation are hard to come by and numbers varied in the media. Additionally, the number of public schools closed post–Hurricane María increased since January 2018. Charter school systems were under serious consideration for implementation as well. In the summer of 2019, Julia Keleher was arrested alongside other high-profile public officials on federal fraud charges, contributing to the eruption of the Verano Boricua or #RickyRenuncia movement.

"Newspaper interview": The poem's epigraph is a quote from the article/interview "Las hermanas que murieron sepultadas en Utuado decían que querían irse juntas" by Mabel M. Figueroa Pérez, published in *El Nuevo Día*.

"If a tree falls": The line "is a kind of silence about injustice" was borrowed from Bertolt Brecht's poem, "To Posterity."

"Rhizomatic": This poem borrows from, was aided and informed by the piece "Many Puerto Ricans fear recovery plan could be greedy land grab" by Hilda Lloréns and Carlos García-Quijano, published in *NY Daily News*.

"Late in the evening": September 21, 2016; September 20, 2017; April 18, 2018; three dates in which Puerto Rico experienced an archipelago-wide power outage.

"Sargassum": This poem borrows from, was aided and informed by the pieces "Record-breaking amounts of sargassum in the Caribbean: What is it and where is it coming from?" by Mickey Charteris, published in *Caribbean Reef Life Blog* and "Masses Of Seaweed Threaten Fisheries And Foul Beaches" by Greg Allen, published in *NPR*.

"Clementines": This poem was inspired by and is in conversation with Mario Benedetti's poem, "Gajos."

"Forgive me when I speak of land": This poem was written after the following lines by Pablo Neruda: "Pardon me, if when I want / to tell the story of my life / it's the land I talk about," translated by William O'Daly. Nonetheless, this poem was written before knowing that Pablo Neruda has been accused of, and confessed to, sexual violence and rape. I have decided to not make mention of him in the body of the poem itself, and to relegate him to the notes so as to unveil here the negotiation between the ethics of attribution and my feminist politics. We have wasted too much time deifying and defending the "art" of those who hurt and continue to hurt us, at the cost of so many. In retrospect, it's unfortunate that this poem is in direct conversation with his own and my apologies to those who consequently experienced hurt. Just as his violences were nonchalantly sprinkled into his work, his name will be merely residual sediment in mine.

"The Governor and the Cock": In 2018, Puerto Rico experienced a record-breaking number of femicides, among other variations of gender violence. Spearheaded by the Colectiva Feminista en Construcción, women, trans, and queer communities throughout the archipelago clamored for the governor of Puerto Rico to sign an executive order and declare a state of emergency in response to the epidemic of gender violence in Puerto Rico. The governor ignored and repressed their claims and demonstrations. A few weeks later, after the US Congress resumed a conversation on prohibiting cock fights in Puerto Rico, the governor immediately retaliated, defending and lobbying for the continuation of this practice on the archipelago.

"A cada lechón le llega su Navidá combativa": The last couplet is made up of two verses from the Puerto Rican aguinaldo "Ese Pobre Lechón." The verses roughly translate into: "You take the pig, kill and skin it. You stick it on a rod, and cook it over open flame."

Acknowledgments

I would like to thank the following online and print publications and platforms in which some of these poems, sometimes earlier or different versions, appeared or are forthcoming:

"Let it tremble," *Disaster Matters: Disasters Matter, House of Nehesi Publishers*, TBA

"Clementines/Mandarinas," *Pigeon Pages NYC*, January 3, 2021

"Noche de San Juan," *Periódico de Poesía UNAM*, July 27, 2020

"Educación," *The Paris Review*, May 22, 2020

"Qué tiemble," *low-fi ardentía,* March 31, 2020

"Home," "Patria," and "Sermon on NYC subway," *The Breakbeat Poets Volume 4: LatiNEXT, Haymarket Books*, April 2020

"Ode to the cacerola combativa/Oda a la cacerola combativa," "In the fissures/En las grietas," and "A cada lechón le llega su renuncia/A cada lechón le llega su renuncia," *Society and Space*, February 24, 2020

"Ode to my studio apartment in Forest Hill, Newark," *Winter Tangerine*, TBA

"A cada lechón le llega su Navidá combativa," *Jamaica Gleaner, Meeting*

Ground: A Special Christmas Collaboration Between Poets of Jamaica and Puerto Rico, December 15, 2019

"A cada lechón le llega su Navidá combativa" and "Partida," *low-fi ardentía*, December 12, 2019

"Late in the evening" and "A hurricane has come and gone. What do we tell our children now?" *Gulf Coast: A Journal of Literature and Fine Arts*, Issue 32.1, March 2019

"Rhizomatic" and "When a tree falls," *Aftershocks of Disaster: Puerto Rico Before and After the Storm, Haymarket Books*, 2019

"D.A. interview" and "Newspaper interview," *Sx Salon*, February 2019

"Patria" and "Cuando un árbol cae," *Revista Trasunto*, March 31, 2019

"Strawberries," *Foundry Journal*, March 2019

"Backyard burial," *Anomaly, Caribbean Folio,* Issue 20, April 2019

"American Airlines Flight #188," *Voces desde Puerto Rico/Voices from Puerto Rico, Red Sugarcane Press*, 2019

"Breath," *Kweli Journal, #PoetsForPuertoRico: Kweli Edition*, October 2018

I want to thank my editor, KMA Sullivan, graphic designer, Alban Fischer, and the Yes Yes Books team, for their keen attention to detail, intentionality, and unwavering belief in my work; for giving my book a home.

I want to thank Colectivo Moriviví and BEMBA PR, for the fierceness of their artwork and cultural-political projects.

I want to thank the following institutions for fostering communities and support systems that have nurtured my growth and voice: *92nd Street Y*, *Voices of Our Nations Arts Foundation*, *Community of Writers*, *Under The Volcano International*, *Las Dos Brujas*, *Moko Writers' Workshop,* and the *Dodge Poetry Foundation*. I'm grateful and honored to have been selected as one of the winners of the *2020 92Y's Discovery Poetry Contest;* and for having received the inaugural *Sandra Cisneros Fellowship* for a Latinx writer of literary promise and leadership from *Under The Volcano International*, and *The Ancinas Family Scholarship* for a writer of Hispanic or Latinx heritage from *Community of Writers*.

I want to thank my MA thesis advisor and poet, Dr. Loretta Collins Klobah, without whose guidance, support, and drive this collection wouldn't have come to fruition.

I want to thank the Department of English of the University of Puerto Rico-Río Piedras, and to express deep gratitude for my professors and mentors, Dr. Dannabang Kuwabong and Dr. Maritza Stanchich, for their generosity, solidarity, and brilliance. I also want to sincerely thank Dr. Rick Swope, Dr. Nick Faraclas, Dr. Nalini Natarajan, and Dr. Yolanda Rivera for their academic, administrative, and moral support.

I want to thank the Department of English of the University of Puerto Rico-Mayagüez, and Dr. Jocelyn Géliga, Dr. Mary Sefranek, and Dr. José Irizarry for creating spaces for our voices to defiantly flourish.

I want to thank maestras Gypsy, Aida Rojas, María Echevarría, Teresa Riestra, and Sheila Riestra for protecting and cultivating the writer in me.

I want to thank the MFA Program in Creative Writing at Rutgers University-Newark, my thesis advisor and mentor Rigoberto González, and my precious MFA poetry cohort (Evan Cutts, Fiona Chamness, Sara Munjack, Spencer Williams, Sydney Choi, Weston Richey, and a special shout out to Lark Omura for holding my work and holding it down with me), for two beautiful years of poetry and community-building.

I want to thank my dear friend, mentor, compa—Raquel Salas Rivera—por meterle ojo, diente y corazón a este manuscrito, and for believing in my work and voice.

Thank you to poet/writer loves and mentors who have seen me and my work, and whose generosity knows no bounds: Ricardo Maldonado, Nicole Delgado, Melinda González, Norma Liliana Valdez, my badass *VONA* cohort (Alfredo Aguilar, April Gibson, Brittany Rogers, JR Mahung, Jubi Arriola-Headley, Malcolm Friend, Mark Maza, Nuri Nusrat, and a special shout-out to Laura Villareal—who's held my work every step of the way) and extended *VONA* familia, my *Community of Writers* familia, my *Under The Volcano* familia, my Las Dos Brujas familia, my *Moko Writers Workshop* familia, Willie Perdomo, Richard Georges, Mariposa Fernández, Ysabel González, Shivanee Ramlochan, Reyna Grande, Essah Díaz, Newark/NYC poets crew, lx corillx del Departamento de Inglés de la IUPI, lx corillx del Departamento de Inglés del Colegio, Rima Brusi, Jessica Muñoz, Haedeh Nazari, Tanya Finklestine, and I know I'm missing many more.

Thank you to the poets and writers I have shared space(s) with. To those whose current outpour transforms me. To those whose words have outlived them and made a home of my mind and body;

José, for the years, love, and transformations—for unconditionally supporting me and my work;

Salima, for all the ways you've loved me, held me, and taught me life;

la familia Powers-Géliga y Fifí, lx corillx de la Alacena Feminista-Luquillo y a todxs lxs compxs de lucha en el archipiélago y en la diáspora—nos tenemos, coño, nos tenemos y vamos por más;

my grandfather Shasha and uncle Dan for the love and support even at a distance;

my father, for witnessing the departure and welcoming the return; my mother, for nurturing my wildness; my sister and her partner, for the laughter and always feeling like home.

PHOTO BY SALIMA HAMIRANI

ANA PORTNOY BRIMMER is a poet and organizer from Puerto Rico. Her debut full-length collection, *To Love an Island*, is out with Yes Yes Books and the Spanish edition is forthcoming from La Impresora. *To Love an Island* was originally the winner of the Yes Yes Books 2019 Vinyl 45 Chapbook Contest. Portnoy holds a BA and an MA from the University of Puerto Rico and is an alumna of the MFA program in Creative Writing at Rutgers University-Newark. She is the winner of the 92Y Discovery Poetry Contest 2020. She is the daughter of Mexican-Jewish immigrants, resides in Puerto Rico, and lives for dance parties and revolution.

Also from YesYes Books

Boat Burned by Kelly Grace Thomas
Helen Or My Hunger by Gale Marie Thompson

RECENT CHAPBOOK COLLECTIONS
Vinyl 45 s
    Inside My Electric City by Caylin Capra-Thomas
    Exit Pastoral by Aidan Forster
    Of Darkness and Tumbling by Mónica Gomery
    The Porch (As Sanctuary) by Jae Nichelle
    Juned by Jenn Marie Nunes
    Unmonstrous by John Allen Taylor
    Preparing the Body by Norma Liliana Valdez
    Giantess by Emily Vizzo

Blue Note Editions
    Beastgirl & Other Origin Myths by Elizabeth Acevedo
    Kissing Caskets by Mahogany L. Browne
    One Above One Below: Positions & Lamentations by Gala Mukomolova

Companion Series
    Inadequate Grave by Brandon Courtney
    The Rest of the Body by Jay Deshpande